SENSE & NONSENSE
ABILITY
true stories are best

Sense & Nonsense Ability
True Stories are Best

Keith Dowell

Copyright © Keith Dowell 2019

ISBN: 978-1-9160938-0-5

Written by Keith Dowell and published by Writersworld, this book is produced entirely in the UK, is available to order from most book shops in the United Kingdom, and is globally available via UK-based Internet book retailers.

Cover Design: Jag Lall

Copy editor: Sue Croft

WRITERSWORLD
2 Bear Close, Woodstock,
Oxfordshire
OX20 1JX
United Kingdom

www.writersworld.co.uk

The text pages of this book are produced via an independent certification process that ensures the trees from which the paper is produced comes from well managed sources that exclude the risk of using illegally logged timber while leaving options to use post-consumer recycled paper as well.

[

DEDICATION AND ACKNOWLEDGEMENTS

I wish to dedicate this book, exclusively . . .

. . . to all human beings everywhere in the world, from every continent; from all of the nations, all of the ethnic groups of every colour, race, creed, religion {or none}, all hot air balloonists, all blood groups including O+ [my favourite but not forgetting A and B], persons of a nervous disposition, pancake tossers, trick cyclists, slug breeders, sports fans, paramedics, dinner ladies who slop some of the food on the plate, giggling giglets, wanton hussies, jovial jesters, Turner Prize rejects, even persistent proctalgiacs and sackbut players {especially all those aged between four and one hundred and four, who buy poetry books}

Without you, nothing much of interest would have happened, ever, anywhere.

And finally, to my family and friends, who taught me the joy of sermocinational prosopopoeia. {What do you think? Sounds alright to me}

P.S. Plus all creatures great and small, including wriggly and crawly things and very small creatures that mite buy poetry books as presents. Thank you.

And thanks for your help: Sue Croft, Jag Lall, and Graham Cook, of WRITERSWORLD.

CONTENTS

PREFACE

My children used to say:

"Tell us some true stories. True stories are best."
So I have based my narrative poems on real
events and real people I have encountered.

A Poem

A poem is some verse or writing, where you
think you know what it means —
but you're not quite sure.
I think.

Art Book

IF you think you are as smart as you look,

read these poems,

then make an art book

to show how the characters look.

ACTS OF WAR - BLAME

I'm sure it would be declared obscene
And definitely against the law
To go out into the street,
And shoot the first person that you saw:
But killers operate in different ways.
There are scientists in laboratories still
Making weapons meant to kill
They say they have some justification.
Now justification there may be
But here we have strange irony
They're getting plaudits for their industry.
And here's the rub that's so derisive
With punishments so divisive
The person in the street, you see,
Is charged with murder in the first degree
The court will dish out retribution: it's all part of
the Constitution
Now those that kill people by proxy and collateral,
And show no emotion just steadfast devotion,
Can end up, with more pay and promotion.
The scientists become justified
By the number of people that have died
I wish they all could show some shame,
It ends with dead bodies, just the same.

ANNETTE BEANIT and Miss Blob in the Jar

There once was a girl called Annette Beanit.
Annette was a girl, who looked delightful,
But beyond the façade was really, really spiteful.
She would ask people their secrets, and then would tell
Blaming others for breakages or a stinky smell.
She picked on those children who couldn't fight back
Being so cunning, she just had the knack.
But dwarfing all that, was her Pièce de Resistance
If you don't know what that is, I'll give you some assistance.

It was the nastiest thing she'd done, by quite a long distance.
The way she did it, she blatantly lied,
And kept on lying until somebody cried.

Now when walking round the school one day,
she saw another child at play,
And with an act so mean and cowardly, she
approached the child and shouted, loudly:
I don't want to cause you grief or sorrow
But, your mother is dead. The funeral's tomorrow.
Later, being questioned on her version,
Said: It was a mistake, I got the wrong person.

When Miss Blob, the headteacher, heard what she had done
She summoned Annette to the office at once,

And said what had happened was really abhorrent.
Annette said the words just came out in a torrent
They were the first words that came into her head
Of course, she didn't mean them: at least that's
what she said.
And no-one in their right mind would wish anyone
dead.

What she had said set Miss Blob a-thinking:
If she had a black eye it would easily show
But what's in her mind: I don't really know.
Miss Blob decided to write a report so she went to
Mrs Beanit to see what she thought.
On meeting Mrs Beanit , Miss Blob really cringed
Not being P C, you'd say, the mother's unhinged
No wonder Annette is mentally phased
Her mother is worse, she is mentally crazed
Miss Blob said: I can't leave it, I must intervene
I'll call for a doctor. He'll see what I've seen.

It seems that Mrs Beanit had a tumour; a lump on
the brain
She had it removed now she's happy and sane
It's made all the difference to Annette they find
She's helpful, caring and honest and kind
The surgeon gave them the culprit,
It's something of a star,
In recognition, it's called:

" Miss Blob in the jar"

Miss Blob

ANDREA LEARNT A LESSON

When people said to Andrea: What do you want to be?
She would always answer: You will have to wait and see.
But her Mother and Father were on some sort of mission
They usually spoke for her, saying: A Medical Physician.
Then, being rebellious, Andrea would add: Or a lady
Electrician.
[It was the sort of thing her parents would pooh – pooh
saying it was a manual job for men, and anyway she
wouldn't know what to do.]
So to prove them wrong, Andrea often carried a
screwdriver and pliers
Hoping one day, someone would say:
Please, can you fix these wires?

It was Andrea's first day at her new school
She'd been told: Obey every rule and do your best, as
they dropped her off, an hour before the rest.
So she wandered in to see what lay in store.
There was an interesting room, with three labels on the
door announcing Cookery, Domestic Science, Home
Economics
It's as if there was some shame
in having Cookery Room as a name.
They changed to make it sound more scientific
But with cookery at the core it's something to deplore.
To call it Cookery Room again would be terrific.

She was feeling rather smug as she removed then re-
wired a plug.

She had finished before anyone came in.

There was one thing; it transpires
They had changed the colours of the wires.
The old arrangement of Red Live and Neutral Black is
what she knew.

She had removed the wires with some aplomb
But, not noting where they're from
When confronted with green /yellow, brown and blue
She could only do the best that she could do.
So, she hoped everything would be fine,
As she went to the yard at nine.

The plug culprit blew the old main fuse, then everything
lost power
The whole building was powerless for nearly half an hour.
They said:
The wiring in that plug, you can't defend
It's a Friday afternoon job at the factory.
Someone was thinking about the weekend.
It's dangerous. It's not satisfactory.

The escapade as a junior electrician taught her a salutary
lesson:
Attend to small things where you need care and precision
That is how she has become her parents' favourite
Physician.

When she told the old story to her best friend Pip,
Phillipa said wisely: A small hole can sink a big ship.

Anthropological Seminar

It's an international anthropological seminar
with delegates from near and far.
We wandered to the coffee break with orders
to integrate
We espied two young ladies from the Native
American delegation
They were cute and we decided: this is our
type of integration.
We thought: if we want to meet them, we must
have a plan
We'll get to know their names as soon as we
can.
So I asked the man beside me:
We'd like to know those two young ladies,
sitting over there
The quiet and coy one and the one with long
black hair
The man said: I do know them, though they're
relatively new.
The quiet and coy one is shy Anne and the
other one is Sue.

Common Sense and Morality

There should be a GCSE in common sense and
morality
And every person in the land,
No matter whether low or grand,
Taught in a plain and simple way,
Should learn and be examined then,
On how to treat our fellow men.

Growing Old

Poor vision, poor audition
Average gustation, olfaction and tactition
With my thermoception I'm always aware
But as you grow older the major bane
Is nociception, it's a real pain.

Being in the Team

It was the original intent to hold a special needs
event
So they would have the chance to play
In a proper soccer tournament
There would be a cup for grabs with medals given
to all the lads
An experience never had, before this day.
Some special needs don't always show
It's sometimes difficult to know
Though each team started in a different way.
Keith's team were lectured how to play
In a fair and sporting way
He said: It really isn't done to argue now with
anyone.
You see, there was a boy named Geoff, who often
argued with the Ref and, if he could not get his
way, would steal the ball and run away.
Keith hinted that it was not done; to foul
opponents just for fun, saying, if rules they did
encroach they'd end up sitting on the coach.
I have to say with some relief that's on the bus
and not on Keith

John's team-talk at the start was slow
His talk accentuated and with signs
He picked his words with clarity and when he'd
finished - just to show
He gave thumbs up to let them know.
On tactics, this would be his last word, for once
on the field he would never be heard

Bill's team talk was the standard kind: the sort at
any game you'd find
Now if you pass, pass to a man. Always do the
best you can
With a kickaround amongst the team, ambulatory
problems could be seen
And those, with medical aplomb, would recognise
some gaits were wrong
Mind, a boy with a withered leg, ironically: ran
round the pitch with speed and glee
The rest, it could not be denied, would struggle
with the running side.

When George's team entered the fray, they
looked the part in every way
But some things were different; it was very clear
When George repeats: I'm over here.

He said: Your first job is to keep them out
Don't shilly-shally or ponce about,
Clear the ball, just get it out.
Hoof it out towards their goal
Then, as if it's a joke to share, said: They can't
score if the ball's up there.
So though slower, with no passing game, their
direct approach had made them scary
The other teams became quite wary

Now in George's school, Patrick, desperate to
play,
Turned up to practice every day, and asked
George if he meant, to take him to the
tournament.
George answered him with some regret:
I know you're keen but here's the rub,
I'd only take you as third sub.
The chance for sure is, you won't play.
Oh, thank you sir, I want to go, to be a sub, I just
don't mind. Oh, thank you sir for being kind.

Eventually the big day came. The Mayor stood up
to play his part, declaring that the games could
start

And later he'd present the cup and see the
winners hold it up
The format was a simple one, each team to play
the other one; and when the points were tallied
up, the two top teams played for the cup.

The final was a dour affair, that ended in a nil-nil
draw
Neither Keith's, nor George's team, could score
Now only penalties would show, which way that
the cup should go.
The crowd by now were so excited: some upset,
some delighted
The teams on the pitch couldn't settle the affair
Locked three goals each thus ending all square
The ref said: From now, if a team gets ahead,
they win the cup; we can all go to bed.

Keith's team went first but the goal was missed
Advantage to George's - a sudden twist
They needed a hero, oh who would it be
There's only two subs left, sub two and sub three
Now George is quite positive; sub two isn't bad
He's scored a few penalties, a confident lad.
They look for him now, it couldn't be worse

He's been taken ill and he's gone to the nurse
So George called on Patrick, the sub number
three

The captain then took him to show him the spot
And when Patrick reached down to feel for the
ball
We guessed he possessed little vision at all
He took one pace back, one pace forward, then
whack
The whole place erupted with jubilant cries and
Patrick was lifted way up to the skies
His friends rushed up to him and patted his back.
Pat was quite chuffed with the goal, it would
seem
But what really thrilled him was –
BEING IN THE TEAM.

Written after a tournament between school leavers from schools for: blind and partially sighted; deaf; physically disabled; and boys with emotional and behavioural problems.

INCLUSIVE

Try to be inclusive
It's not really that elusive.
Don't use up all your patter
Talking to those you think that matter.
Talk to anyone you know that's friendly
And wants to have a natter; and their say.
For you might be the excluded one, one day.

IF YOU COULD CHANGE A DAY

If today always came again the day after
tomorrow, would you want to repeat the
laughter and the sorrow
If given the choice with no reverse
Would you accept it again, chapter and verse
Or would you gamble and change it
For better or worse

Biddy has Dyslexia

Biddy has Dyslexia and nobody knew
When it came to work with words, she was really in a stew.
She knew all the answers, but she couldn't write them down
So to divert attention, she acted like a clown.
When the other children saw this
They thought that she was thick
But an expert came into school and recognised the trick.
She knows all the answers. She could tell you pretty quick.
He said: She's an intelligent girl, who needs a little aid
And very soon, some of her work is going to be displayed.
Since the diagnosis her confidence just grew
And at last she is showing what she knew, she knew, she knew.

THE BIRD AT BEST VIEW

I had a landlady. Her name Mrs Adey.
Her house in the North East of England.
I went back one night and had quite a fright
It was after midnight, I could still see a light.
I'd been down to the pub for a pint and some grub
The lights on for sure as I opened the door
I thought: poor Mrs Adey that lovely old lady
Has fallen and broken her pelvis
As she danced to her CD of Elvis.

I whispered: My dear, I'm here, can you hear?
With a small broken voice came an answer
I can't go to bed 'til that creature has fled
I'm stuck in the kitchen, the bird's in the lounge
I need to get through: What can I do?
This little old lady who won't hurt a fly
Said: Kill it, destroy it, and started to cry
Don't worry, I'll move it, there's no need to harm it
As soon as I find it, I'll release the varmint

Then out came the bird, I don't know from where
[My mother once told me Bats fly into your hair]
I could see why some people would easily scare.
Now the bird, a small sparrow, flew to and fro
With no open windows and nowhere to go

Has it gone yet? she cried. Won't be long I replied
As I opened the windows and door
But the poor little mite flew again and again
All in vain at the closed window pane.
I took off my coat and waved it about
But it seemed unwilling to be ushered out
The bird flew back and then I lost track.
I thought it had flown, in all the confusion
But I soon realised it was all an illusion.

Can I come out now? Can I come through?
You are my hero to do what you do.
I'd be stuck in the kitchen if it wasn't for you.
Twas then a faint chirrup. I wasn't quite sure
I thought she'd not heard it, but slam went the door.
The little old lady had started to fret
Locked in the kitchen and clearly upset
With the old Tempus Fugit, I felt a real twit
I needed a logical plan, a remit:
Moths fly from the dark so why not a lark [or a sparrow].
First an hour in the dark. Blow that for a lark.
After an hour and a third I located the bird
It was in the back of the settee. Now I'd better explain:

The old settee had a sacking back and in one corner
it was lacking a tack
So the sacking fell back and the bird
Saw the gap in the sacking where the tack was
lacking.

After an hour and a third I'd located the bird
But the settee was wrapped all around it.
So what could I do? I was in quite a stew.
The road was the place to release it.
The settee was heavy, the settee was bulky
But this was no time to be sullen and sulky
With muscle and might and masculine feat
I managed to drag said sofa to street
With one-third on path and two-thirds on street
I stopped to take heed and listen for tweet

At about half past four, along came the Old Bill
Saw settee and me as they cruised down the hill
They crept up behind me, said: What have we here?
Help had arrived, I near shed a tear
It might sound absurd but I'm seeking a bird
Now who is this bird that you're looking for?
They asked, then sniggered and made a guffaw
It's in the settee I replied;
And the old lady's locked in the kitchen inside.

With that, the mood became quite tense
The cops said: This is some offence
I told the cop: The bird's in there.

As he peeled back the sacking, the sparrow flew out
I jumped in the air with a whoop and a shout
The neighbours joined in with generous applause
They'd been watching events through windows and
doors
The distressed Mrs Adey was formally released
And all animosity from the officers ceased
There was just time left, for the boys in blue
To assure Mrs Adey that the bird had flew.
Mrs Adey was sorry the bird was ill
She said I'd have left it, if I only knew.
A literate neighbour tried to explain,
While the poor little sparrow flew back in again.

Bob and Kitty

There were some siblings called Bob and Kitty
Brother and sister, more's the pity
Now Bob was a slob with a tremendous gob
With an horrendous habit of spitting and flobbing.

Now if you are a person of a sensitive nature
I'll describe flobbing in a more delicate way.
It was mucus, germs and nasal secretions
Propelled as projectiles and done for display

Now Kitty was pretty and witty, intelligent and nice
If you wanted to befriend her, you wouldn't think
twice
It's a pity she's stuck with a brother like Bob
Will he always go spitting and act like a slob?
Bob got her to flob once just as a trial
She quit after a minute: it wasn't her style.
Her spitting, if any, was measured not manky
Aimed discretely, into a delicate white hanky.

Bob would kick puppies and push over Grannies
And if there were rich kids, he'd push over their
Nannies.
He often begged clothes, which he got by the dozen
Pretended he bought them, then sold them to his
cousin
Sometimes Kitty sneaks out to rescue some kittens

And if they have cold paws, she knits them some mittens
Then about midnight she embroiders some dresses
They seem to be made out of love and caresses
Then at dawn she is baking some cakes of renown
To carry to the orphanage the other side of town.
If you want to describe them, in terms very simple –
Bob, a nasty and germy pimple, and Kitty, a cute little dimple.

In the town where Bob lived, you knew where he'd been
The pavements were covered in yellow and green
And when he had a cold or flu
The shades and colours grew and grew
One day he had a nosebleed, and before you knew it
The flag of Canada. It had to be seen
Two red stripes and a maple leaf between.
It wasn't long before he reached his zenith
He could spit a model of Paris or Venice.

Bob

The people in the town said: Do something quick.
This disgusting boy is making us sick.
Now the local council met when the moon was blue
In fact they hadn't met since two thousand and two
But now there were kids of nought to four
Who wandered outside and were stuck to the floor
The townsfolk wanted more protection

So they threatened the council with de-selection
And, thinking expenses would go in the same
direction,
They passed a byelaw they never had before Under:
Protection of the Pavement Act 1834
There now was a law for their protection
So that anyone accused of mucus projection
Gets a fine and a month's detention.

Bob saw this as a challenge and said: I don't give a
damn
I'll spit in the street as often as I can
They'll have to catch me, that's a fact
I'll just get cunning, not get caught in the act.
However, punishment came in a strange salutary way
One day Bob noticed his spit was red
The doctor was called and he was sent to bed
The doctor called the family in and said:
Bad Luck,
With all that spitting he has ruptured his cluck.

It has taken a long time for Bob to come to terms
That he was upsetting people and spreading germs,
So he's established a charity, calling it:
Only a Git Would Spit . . . I Quit.
Kitty thought the name should be
Everyone Can Change; Give Them Time and See.

BOG STANDARD: Cyrille and Roderick

At the Bog Standard Paper Mills, Cyrille had one role,
As the Sub-manager of Grading, Buying, Design,
Manufacture, and Quality Control.
The Boss, Mr Bottomley, had told him:
We have to make the perfect toilet roll.
But it better not cost a lot for sure.
Make it cheap and we'll make a lot more.
So Cyrille designed a paper of the time; glassy on one
side and the other side like grit.
And thinking folks would love it, he called it: Cherish It.

At the Excelsior Paper Mill the other side of town
They brought in Roderick Draper, who'd been many
years in paper, who designed a product soft as
Eiderdown.
[Cyrille said to his Boss: No need to frown. Ignore
Roderick's ideas, he's just a clown.]
But Rod saw the glossy, glassy, and saw the gritty grit,
Saw that it was rubbish and just got rid of it.
Then with a revolutionary feat so neat,
Took the soft paper and made a double sheet,
Declaring he could now relax, his life's work was
complete.

They still make toilet rolls at Bog Standard, but
the purpose is not quite so plain,
People now compare them to Roderick's and send them
back again,
All with an attached envelope with a letter to complain.
Bog Standard recycle all the paper and make a few
toilet rolls just the same, but have spotted a
new-niche-business making envelopes for those
who complain.
It seems more people complain now and claiming for
everything is a popular trend,
Solicitors' adverts encourage them {it drives me round
the bend}.
Now Cyrille's latest offering is a winner all the way
An envelope that's printed: "Complaint. Do not throw
away."
Mr Bottomley only thinks toilet rolls, so it's driving him
insane, seeing Cyrille's advert, by his name.

'Bog Standard: Don't put up with it.
Write in and complain.'

Brexit in our street

If Brexit happened in our street
With neighbours I have known for years.
Yes, years full of laughter and tears.
I would say to my neighbours:
This is my house, this is my place,
I don't need you now so don't show your face.
I've got new friends that live on a distant estate
I'll do things with them: they'll reciprocate.
But one day while making tea,
I realise there's no sugar for me,
So I go round next door; with cap in hand, with
cup in hand.
The next-door neighbour says: None to spare
The other neighbours say: We don't care

You thought you were clever in making a split

You've made your own bed, now lie in it.

Can't ya see I'm makin' a call?

Mum, will Santa bring a present for me?

I dunno, wait an' see
Now shut up, I'm makin' a call.
Is that you, Cind, I'm in the store
I've seen these new jeans I ain't seen before

Mum, who ya talkin' to?

Oh, that's just our Billy, I'll soon shut 'im up
What time are ya goin', I'd like ta go wiv ya?
An' Sylv an' Krystal are goin' there too
Yeh, don't time fly, she's turned twenny two

Mum, what's that thing on top of the tent?

Ya not tellin' me it's the rent that she spent.
Yeh, I'm goin' tomorra, I'm 'avin a trim

Oh, Mum, look over there, I can see Santa's in

I warned ya, Billy, wiv ya whinin' an all
You won't get no present, not even a ball
Can't ya see I'm makin' a call?

Charles Aggis-Cells: he drinks and probably smells

I had a former teacher, Charles Aggis-Cells
People in the neighbourhood say: he drinks and
probably smells.
He always looks unkempt and wears old-fashioned
clothes
Why has he let himself get like that? Nobody knows.

I met him in the Market Square, one Saturday in
May, explaining, I had come back, just for the day.
He seemed really interested to know what I had done
Since I had left the school in nineteen ninety-one.
He said: If you've time, do you fancy a beer?
I'm meeting a friend in the pub over here.
Now, you sit down, in that seat over there
What can I get you? I said: I don't care.
He brought two half pints of the cheapest you'd find
Said he couldn't afford Reponi. He hoped I didn't
mind.

Then his friend, Jack, joined us and started to chat
About nothing particular, just this and that
When Charles asked all about me, about my home
and wife
We spoke all about me but never about *his* life.

Then Charles said: I'm sorry, I really have to leave.
I've got a meeting with the Mayor; would you believe.

As Charles walked away, Jack said: You wouldn't be impressed
I suppose if you look at him, you'd say he's shabbily dressed
Though his clothes are from the charity shop
They are always clean and pressed.
I know he buys half pints and dresses cheaply as he can
Because most of his money goes to a clinic, in Sudan.
He pays for a clinic, as modern as you will find.
It gives treatment and operations to stop people going blind.
He sends his own money and collects money too
He always says, it is the least that he can do.
For more than fifteen years now, I think you will find
Thirty thousand people he has saved from going blind.

Now that is no small beer.

Our Home

A Christmas poem

> Saviour lovely, Saviour fair,
> Guide us into your loving care;
> God attend us, we all can share
> In our home town here,
> A gift from precious Mary.
>
> His life began in a manger bare,
> At Christmas time,
> In Bethlehem;
> His love spread out to east and west,
> To north and south:
> Jesus, Jesus,
> Lo, we come in hope and joy; He leads us.
>
> Blessed Saviour, Blessed Child,
> Born in a manger with mother mild;
> God begat thee, both undefiled,
> To our home here,
> A love from precious Mary.
>
> His life began in a manger bare,
> At Christmas time,
> In Bethlehem;
> His love spread out to east and west,
> To north and south:
> Jesus, Jesus,
> Lo, we come in hope and joy; He leads us.

If You're Crook, Come to Cook

We have been travelling by train and the journey is
terrific
It's the Land of Oz and the train's the Indian Pacific
You've been a long time on the train when you hit the
Nullarbor Plain
And it's plain to see the track is straight –
There is not one single bend for 297 miles from start to
end
Now the train is slowing down and you see a little town
You take another look and you see the town's called
Cook
Then a sign says: If you're crook come to live in Cook.
I'll explain now what it means, as it's not all that it
seems
They are saying anyone who's sick should move here
real quick.
If ill people come to live here, Government services
must appear.
A condition getting worse might bring a Doctor and a
nurse.
You see, there's a doctor's surgery of a sort, a gaol and
a law court, a shop, a school, a bar and railway station
The only thing not found are people walking round.
With two, it's the smallest population.
It is rather a sad story if you remember its former glory

Now a train stops here twice a week, for a twenty-minute break
The couple with the shop take all the money they can make.
And they don't work off their socks – people throw money in a box.
This job must be unique, they work a forty-minute week.
With all it has going for it, you'd think some folks would stay
But they stay for a short time and then they move away.
The passengers on the train said: Why don't you come and live here, you're always telling others?
I said: With my reputation, where would I get my lovers?
Now the train is leaving, we wave goodbye to George and Anne
Leaving them alone here would have been most unkind but with anthropophobia, they don't really mind.
If we look at the reason why most other people won't stay, ironically the reason is other people won't stay.
It seems the thing we cherish most, are friendships we can share.
I wonder how long it will be before no-one's living there.

DAVE

There was a boy, Dave, almost thirteen,
Lived with his mother in Badger Green
And when he went to school that day
Was sobbing, sobbing all the way.
Though friends were there to add some cheer,
He cried and cried, tear after tear.
Near-teenage boys, I think you'd say, are quite reluctant
to display their emotions in this way.
The teacher, later, observed the boy
And thinking it was just a ploy,
A ploy to avoid the present session:
A double mathematics lesson,
Ignored him.
But when the sobbing would not stop
The teacher then, being most concerned,
Put into play the things he had learned
at a teachers' course called: Teenage Angst.
So that Dave was less on show, he moved him
into the back row
But the others complained that they'd lost track
Because of the sobbing from the back.
The teacher thinking he'd got worse
Sent Dave off, to see the nurse.
When Dave had gone, one of his friends said:
I know what's wrong. I will explain.
This morning when Dave went for the bus
Patches, his dog, saw the gate ajar

Ran in the road and was hit by a car
And if on its own that wasn't enough
The driver got out, and without saying sorry,
Kicked the body under a lorry.
Then Dave's Mum appeared, as if by magic, saying:
Patches is dead, don't make such a fuss
Now go to school, get on that bus.
Another friend then chipped in to say:
To make it worse it's Dave's birthday.
This was his first day as a teen,
A circumstance both sad and mean.
Then added: No wonder he is sad and glum
With no card or present from his Mum.
Someone said: His mother don't care,
yet he still loves his mother, that isn't fair.
They all agreed it was really hard, so maths was stopped
and they all made a card.
Next day, Dave did bring a card to school
A card produced under duress
And scrawled across The First Noel, read:

'Burfday greetins to my luvly sun
Wiv lots and lots of luv from Mum'

The wrong spellings didn't mean a thing;
The insincerity was king.

Devon (1)

Dining al fresco at the patio table. Dodging the
showers as we were able.
Hearing more traffic go coughing by: breathing the
fumes that would make us cry.
Then I saw a picture of Dorset or Devon,
With a cottage I'd adore, with roses round the
door,
A quieter place there's never been
A motor car could not be seen
And I honestly swear you could smell the fresh air
It almost looked like Heaven.
My wife saw the picture and said; I adore that
little thatched cottage with flowers round the door.
Then what happened next was all of a mist:
I raised up my arm and banged down my fist.
My wife was quite worried, she'd not seen me
like this,
Well, not for a long time since I gave her a kiss.
I think that we've lived here quite long enough
We're going house-hunting, so pack all your stuff.
We're finding a home down in the South West,
Is Dorset or Devon or Cornwall the best?
And Rosey, although taken aback, shot into the
house and started to pack, saying:
I really, really want to view the house that we'll be
moving to.
So we travelled first to Devon, to see if it really
was like Heaven.

Devon (2)   Finding the House

There was a place in a Devon town, a land agency of small renown.
Run by twin sisters Clack and Clack
Not in the High Street, but round the back.
The office not a grand affair,
But business enough to keep them there.
We entered in the dust and gloom, to see the pictures in the room.
A farm and cottages were on display,
But right next to a motorway.
As we were about to say goodbye, Marjorie Clack caught my eye,
And ushered us into another room, to show us a picture in sepia hue, of an old house called Odicombe.
It was a grand old Georgian stack with loads of windows front and back.
Then we were just about to say: Oh, do you have a viewing day?
When Marilyn the other twin said: Why don't you view it straightaway?
They sent us off with keys to view, armed with the picture in sepia hue.
She said: Drive past the church by the Horse & Groom
You'll see the turn to Odicombe.
The lane was narrow, the lane was dirty, we arrived at a crossroads at about nine-thirty, with no sign saying which way to go.

As luck would have it a man named Mike, came up to the crossroads on his bike.
I wound down the window and beckoned him forth.
I said: To tell us the way would be awfully kind.
He said: Wurr yer goin', wurr yer lookin ta find?
We showed him the picture in sepia hue.
Oh, I know the ol' house, I know wurr ya goo.
Then starting the sentence with ooarrgh,ooarrgh,
Said: Turn left at crossroads, it ain't very far.
So I wound up the window for the route was now plain,
Then more tapping on the window, it's that Mike man again.
So I wound down the window to hear what he'd say.
Now I forgot to mention, you must think that I'm thick.
If you turn right at the crossroads, you'll get there real quick.
So I wound up the window and scratched at my head, trying to interpret what the old man had said.
I'd wound up my window, it was driving me insane, when a tap on the window, it was Mikey Boy again.
So I wound down the window, feeling vexed and perplexed
It was all a confusion, and you know what happened next.

The old man lifted up his arm and pointed
straight ahead.
I suppose you know you can go straight on.
I really should have said.
But if I was goin' that way, that way I wouldn't go.
Pot'oles.

Devon (3)   In the House

I'm excited, I'm happy, I'm starting to grin
I turn the key quickly, I'm letting us in.
Now the porch was so spacious: the hall was as
well
But what we first noticed: the horrible smell
Whatever the smell is it's really a hummer
It smells like wet dogs in a tent in the summer
The sheen of the green on the walls looks like
gloss
On closer inspection it turns out to be moss.
Rosey's disappointment is now showing, I fear,
I say: Think. Just use your imagination my dear.
We could have this place spotless – in a month –
or a year
The floor is all manky: it's skiddy a bit
On closer inspection it's covered in – I don't want
to be coarse so I'm calling it grit.
We noted the wiring, the plumbing, the sink, the
floors and the ceilings, the walls and the stink
The list is so long, there's some I won't mention
So we climb up the stairs with some apprehension
Now, with the bedrooms, I'm playing a hunch

I guess that the Master will be best of the bunch
The door is flung open, we're looking around
My wife is so thrilled with the thing that she's found
A huge Adam fireplace in marble, plus tiles
At last there is something that's causing her smiles
Now this will be cosy and add lots of cheer:
Imagine this room with a real fire in here
This is the thing she's loving the most, imagining
supper with crumpets and toast.
But now I am pensive and looking aloof.
I say: If you look upwards, you'll see there's no roof.
The dream, it has ended, but she said with some pride
It hasn't worked out but at least we have tried
We've both learned a lesson: Still reach out with intent
but if you can't make it, then just be content.
I know with my old house, I've not got a lot
Shucks, not living in Odicombe, I don't give a jot
I've still got my husband and he's handsome and hot
I was so proud of Rosey, although she was shattered, Saying
We still loved each other –
And that's all that mattered.

Farewell to a Child

The lyricists wrote in songs I knew
That breaking up is hard to do
A lover's tiff could end romance
But promise of a second chance
Made losing love a temporary affair
Parting friends may be upset
Their words and actions leave regret
But truly, time will soften pain
And friends once lost can still be friends
again.

But there is an anguish never reconciled
The parting of a parent from a child
The time of parting on that fateful day
Brings nightmares that will never go away
Some part, searching for a better life
Some part, freeing them from strife

But some will leave to go a heavenly way
And find a final resting place to stay.
It is impossible to gauge the pain
Of never seeing, being with your child again
With real feelings masked by outward grace
Hid by the curtain of a stoic face
While inwardly the bitter tears will flow
As only people who have known, will know.

There is a breaking of a bond of love
Felt here on earth and heaven above.

KCG Dowell
December 2018

Three Ladies Came to Stay

Three ladies came to stay: three mothers.
    Three ladies came to stay: Bosnian, Croat and
    Serb.
    Their journey an act of reconciliation.
Brought together, a quarter of a century after the
    event
Tied by a common bond.
    In their own homes, attacked by their
    neighbours.
They cried as they told me: they fled whilst the
    children died.
    Returning when the killing stopped; burdened
    with guilt and anger.
I took them to Stratford: they mingled like tourists
    do.
We wandered round Warwick at a tranquil pace:
    talking and smiling.
    I saw a glimpse of hope: hatred turn to love.
At Kenilworth we stood in Echo Meadows.
    The castle shone orange-buff across the valley.
    The sun shone. The sky was azure blue.
I shouted 'Oi' and 'Echo', towards the castle walls.
    Just a moment later the walls returned my
    calls.
They shouted in three languages,
    I asked what they had called.

They each replied, "Our children's names"
  And said they would enjoy these games.
  If they'd been here at all.
I asked if they still thought of them
  They answered straightaway.
We only think about them - Every Hour - of Every
  Day.

Different groups went on tours with me. Not all witnessed the worst of the war but for some it was different. The poem gives a general idea of their feelings at the time.

The background of many of these ladies was very distressing. One lady saw her neighbours kill her three children and husband after a spell of ethnic cleansing. She had to escape to rescue her elderly parents. She could not return home for nine years. Another who came was nominated for the Nobel Peace Prize. Both have promoted peace, forgiveness and reconciliation. I took some of the ladies on trips around Warwickshire to relax and forget for a while the intensity of the Touch of Hope workshops. They shared each other's stories and proved there is always hope of reconciliation.

Update
  The town where one of the ladies lives has brought all the national and ethnic groups into one new school.

Froggy Bill

There was a boy, who just for fun
Would shout abuse at everyone
And, much to their astonishment,
Rejected their admonishment.
He said he was just having fun.
And when he saw he was being chased,
He quickly ran away with haste.

Bill, the boy, was quite a fool,
he always ran home straight from school,
the very self-same way.
One day he was caught, when about to flee,
But large as life, said: You can't touch me
I'll call the police and you will see
I'll say that you are hurting me.
This ploy works without fail.
You'll be the ones to go to gaol.

Then all the neighbours at Blackberry Hill
Had a meeting saying they'd had their fill
Of that nauseating, foulmouthed kid called Bill.
So on Monday they drew up their plan of action
Hoping it would work to their satisfaction.
Across the street just after four, old clothes and gloves
they wore.
They built a fence five feet high and copiously covered
it in a bright green dye.
Then along came Bill shouting abuse, with no mental
problems there was no excuse
He said:

Easy peasy, lemon squeezy I'll climb over that fence.
It'll be dead easy.

Mummy at home vented some spleen saying:
What have you done and where have you been?
You and your clothes are covered in green.
Into the tub went clothes and Bill but in the morning
they were grass-green still.
Off to school next day and his mother went too,
saying:
Please excuse my Billy with his grass-green hue,
Especially as the other kids are dressed in pale blue.

A few washings later, it could easily be seen that his
uniform was blue but Billy was still green.
But it made no difference, he shouted and swore
Just as many times as he did before.
Someone had to do something, there had to be a cure.

Now a little girl in school one day, who'd returned from
being ill,
Without meaness or malice, shouted:
Look at froggy Bill!
The other kids thought this was fun and started to chant
in unison.
And when they started singing:
Froggy, Froggy, Froggy, Froggy Bill
They went on ad nauseam, it made him feel quite ill.

After a while the whole story worked out
Mummy talked to Bill and she didn't scream or shout;
I've got a cloth with soap, just a teeny-weeny bit, but
if you're still profane, I'll wash your mouth with it.

Bill then enquired the meaning of profane
It means irreverent or impious,
I see they're words you've not met yet, So
I'll eschew obfuscation with an easier explanation:
Remember there are unkind and rude words that make
people upset
You could easily say something that later you regret
Think of the time they called you Froggy Bill
You didn't like it, did you? It nearly made you ill
At that moment Bill replied: Profanity I will not do
And Mummy said: Oh, William, my paragon of virtue.

SARAJEVO

If only he'd had a satnav:
the driver.
One Archduke and millions
die peacefully in their beds.
Maybe

In between or Out of the Box

Official Application says: Don't bother me with letters, you
can do it all online.
The rhetoric is easy but reality's a swine.
Online I seem to fall between the boxes.
You want to register your child for the local nursery:
You would rather write a letter.
But, on the phone they say it's better
If you start doing everything online.
Now they have you in their system and to make sure that
You're listening they are sending you a warning
Saying, that you'll add to global warming
If you persist in writing letters
And they really should know better:
As they're sending all the warnings out – by letter.
Now online you have to start with the Data Gathering part.
They want name, age and address in anticipation.
You've no time to relax as you give them all the facts,
Including sexual orientation.
You are ticking all the boxes and it's going swimmingly
Until you CANNOT TICK A BOX;
You're a Dad age fifty-three.
Age over fifty hasn't got a box to tick in.
Stuck without an answer, you just don't exist or fit in.
So to counter so much ignorance and showing no remorse
You tick box 'under sixteen' to add a little sauce.
In this age of technology with boxes by decree
There must be other in-betweens or outsides,
Just like me.

It's Mine

It won't be long before we see, some mid-ocean entity
Someone, who claims to be the owner of a patch of
sea
They'll say: I've registered it quite legally.
They'll want to claim and say: this patch of sea is mine
If you keep out, it will be fine; but if you enter without
cause
We could end up with fighting wars.
Just think this logic applied to land
No one on earth gave God a hand in making this
world.
Now leasing land would be more fair
People and nations would still have land
But this would make them be aware
And understand, it's not their land.
It's land that's in their care.

Because my ancestors won a war in 1463
Wouldn't mean I own the land in perpetuity
There is no reason or rhyme,
To think: The Divine has made it mine.

Now if I said: I own the Sun
And now I'm taxing everyone who uses it for heat or
light

They'd say: the Sun is, but you're not too bright.
You can't do that it doesn't belong to you.
Yet people on earth think it's alright
To start a war and cause a fight, over a piece of
real estate
That wouldn't be classed even as third rate,
With no minerals or fertility, but because they
say:
It belongs to me
It's mine.

THE DOG RESCUE CENTRE

They leer and sneer; it's all veneer.
They will cajole; they're on parole.
You think it is logic;
they use their magic.
You think you're smart;
they break your heart.
While you're perusing;
they do the choosing.

Jacky

Every morning Jacky looks at her Mickey Mouse
watch
It's surprising most mornings it's about ten
o'clock
And if it is rainy or a bright sunny day, she goes
to the shops that are not far away.
Jacky goes there, with her best friend Janine
Who, since yesterday, she has not seen

Now it's not long after they arrive there
They are looking at bibs in the new
Mothercare
Then after an hour of looking around
They go to the caff where they're usually found
The caff has armchairs and a comfy settee
They sit there each morning with a big pot of
tea
If they want to stay there, longer than they
oughta,
They take their own teabags and ask for more
water.
And there's a routine – that's if they are able –

to collect the spare milk that's been left on a table.
They talk about the usual things: like single men and wedding rings
Jacky is married: Janine is not.
It doesn't seem to matter a jot.
They both share interest in similar things
Like single men and wedding rings.

One day Jacky gave Janine a big surprise
I've a hair appointment. You'll not believe your eyes
I've got an appointment, at ten to two. I'm having my hair dyed pink and blue.

Now every other Thursday at half-past two
She goes to the Job Centre, for a job interview
To look for a job that she could do.
She once had a job but she got the sack
She'd been there an hour and they sent her back.
The follow-up report was blunt, I guess:
Where it said: Rate her. It said: Use-less
Though underneath in brackets it did atone:

[She tried her best, no fault of her own.]
Every other Thursday the Centre says: That's it
There's no job for you, you remain on Benefit.

People say: That Jacky, she hasn't half got
some gall,
She's on State benefit and she doesn't work at
all.
Now I see a paradox. Is this really fair?
Look at my example and then compare.
Lady Poshsocks, who inherited a very large
estate
Got quarter of a million government subsidies,
of late.
Yet people treat her differently.
The reason; I don't know why.
While one lives a life of luxury
The other just gets by.

JIM AND FLO

Jim Roger was an old codger, they called him
Mr Fixit
If there was something broken, he'd stop and
want to fix it
His wife Florence was a bossy old moo
She was always telling Jim what he ought to do.
But Jim was clever enough to know:
Never go against the flow or Flo.
Now the hotel breakfast was rather fine,
It was the help-yourself, the buffet kind
Flo told Jim what to get and how to get it
I can't wait all day, is what she used to say
Jim did this without complaining,
I think it was his servant training.
But the toaster was slower than a tax rebate
And Flo wasn't the sort to hang around and wait
She said to Jim: I want it and I want it now
Under his breath Jim said: Silly old Moo
{Don't even think it]
When no-one was looking, he peered round the back
The toaster dials said HEAT and TRACK
So he increased both dials as far as he could
Then casually entered the bread as one should.

When the black and blue smoke came out from
the back
He looked for his table and quickly headed back.
Now with everyone spluttering and trying not to
Cough, that's when all the fire alarms went off.
The whole hotel obeyed the fire alarm, both
chapter and verse
With staff and guests safe, it could have been
worse.
Mr Fotheringill the manager said:
I don't really know who the culprit might be
But no harm is done, the fire's out you see.
Then, the handyman, Doug Iles, said it was
the toaster dials
Over time they must have slipped, but now I've
sorted it.
The lady next to Flo said: I don't agree with Mr Iles:
I reckon some fool has fiddled with the dials.
If I was married to that Wally
It would drive me off my trolley
I'd kick him in the rump and take him down the dump.
Then Flo looked at Jim and had to agree,
I wonder,
just wonder,
who the Wally could be.

Jokey type things

How is your new Italian Restaurant going, Angelo?
Not too good, with this Winter weather.
Don't worry, it will soon be Spring. Things cannelloni get better.

What is it, Dentist?
Your mouth looks like a piano keyboard, with all those black teeth.
Will I have to have some out?
Yes, B flat and D sharp.

You said that you had discovered a new heavenly body with a coma and tail, but it wasn't true was it? What have you got to say about that?
No comet.

Can you tell us about your new book, Enlightenment?
No comment.

I fluctuate between diarrhea and constipation. I think the medical term is Bipoolar.

Waiter, the menu says a trio will be playing: a piano, a violin, and a sello.
No sir, that's chello – ch.ch.ch. The c is pronounced ch. I thought everyone knew that. Now, would you like a starter?
Yes, I think I'll have the Chorn on the Chob.

My wife wants to change her name by deed poll to Hazel
Brazil.
What is she, some kind of nutter?

What is it, Sherlock?
I think you will find it's a piece of human gut.
How did you know that, Sherlock?
Alimentary, my dear Watson.

My parents are in the iron and steel business:
My Mother sits at home and irons;
My father goes out and – looks after the foundry.

Dad, there's a duck at the door with a bill.
Tell him I'll pay later.

Your brother talks like a donkey.
Ee-aw ee-aw ee-always talks like that.

Is that your Tristran playing a mouth organ?
No, it's 'ar Monica.

Don't you know any James Bond characters?
No.

Don't you know the names of any small creatures?
Might.

I haven't done my philosophy homework, I didn't have
the books.
Did you ask John or Ergo? I know Ergo 'ad some.

More Jokey Type Things

It's an author, who writes about the social landscape of the age.
Who the Dickens is it?

He's written a book about his discovery of a new wonder bendy material. He's hoping to make a lot of money out of it.
What's it called?
Great Flexpectations.

The child is staying with her schizoid Aunty and her psychotic Uncle. They are acting in loco parentis.

There goes that Maths teacher telling his kids off again: I've told you not to do that "n" times. Do I have to tell you "n" plus one?

Today I saw these youths with pit bull dogs. They were ugly, vicious, aggressive, with filthy yellow teeth. The dogs were not too pleasant either.

I've got a brother who lives in Mortem in Devon. He's a postman. One day some letters were destroyed. They had to have a Mortem post enquiry to find out what had happened.

I would recommend any Wizard out there looking for a wife, to subscribe to Which magazine.

Did the Greeks and Romans race horses?   Yes

What about pigeons, did they race pigeons?
I'm sure Homer did.

I know it's not looking too bad but do you think we should refurbish the Art Deco furniture?

I reckon if it's not Baroque don't mend it.

That's a hard question. Are you a liar?

"I am just not strong anymore." That was quote of the weak.

"Well, that's another twenty-four hours over." That was quote of the day.

I've done a lot of auditions lately. I tried for a part in Pinocchio but they said I was too wooden. I tried for a part in The Life of Jane Austen. They said my acting lacked pride, but I think they were prejudiced. I did get a part in the panto, Dick Whittington. I think they liked me. They kept shouting, "bring back the cat" as I left the stage.

I wanted something to do with the kids during the holidays. Someone suggested Punch and Judy. The punch part was easy but there was no-one at A and E called Judy.

That car salesman keeps telling you about the most powerful engines for towing. I know he's all torque.

June

It has been almost a year of bitter tears and pain
Now June must face the world again
Hoping for sympathy and care
From all her friends, who are living there.
She saw some friends, but some just walked on by
Though one or two just managed to say Hi
And after they had passed she heard them say:
Her husband left her on her wedding day
So from then on, she would be known, as:
June, the one that lives there on her own.
June, the one that lives there all alone.
Alas, those labels were replaced quite soon
And now, unthinkingly, she's known as:
June, the one whose husband left her, on her honeymoon.

Just for a Lark

Just for a lark,

We went down to the park.

She was commoner than air:

But I didn't care.

I hadn't a clue .

She said, Here's what you do.

It wasn't too bad.

The quins call me Dad.

Now when I go to the park:

It's not for a lark.

I study the flowers for hours and hours.

After defending a young Asian mother and two small children from a racist thug, on a long tram journey in Rome. Written in the epic style with Charlotte the Rebel at Oxford.

KEITH the RESILIENT

If I can see a person in danger or difficulty
When in Rome or at Rome
I can intervene and shield them from harm.
I can be the key to their endeavours
And get them out of their mess.
I, Keith the Resilient,
With my body as a shield and my heart as my calling
Can with inner strength defend the helpless
When I see those in need of aid
I can go the distance and retrieve what was lost
Restoring back the peace.
I offer up myself to bear the pain
Forced by the tattoo bearer, that ugly-looking chap,
Who tried to hurt the lady and the babes.
He spat hatred words at me and would not let go
I stood alone, when no-one else would.

MEDICAL HISTORY

In olden days you had to be wary;
Going to the Docs was pretty scary.
If we scrutinize medical history, we can see that it's a
mystery, anyone survived at all.
There was little training then, of course, you could treat a
person if you could shoe a horse.
To see what happened we'll take a look,
By inspecting notes from Doctors' Books.

This guy was carried to the surgery
And a kid followed on, just to see
A huge guy ,he was seven foot three
It seemed this kid had lobbed a stone
And before you know it, there was a groan.
Down the guy began to fall: the lump on his head, like a
football.
The Doc said: Watch where you're throwing, son.
That rock you threw could have hit anyone.
The kid, showing off, said: Throwing? Not me. I've got a
sling here, can't you see. You'd better write his obituary.

This Roman guy just staggered in
Complaining of a sharp stabbing pain
Doc said: You've had an accident. Been playing with that
old dagger again?
Now, the guy had been attacked, he said,
And they certainly did a good job.

When I said: What Brute did that?
You could see he wanted to sob.
Just then this guy's mate came in, a skinny bloke named
Cas
He had a lean and hungry look.
I think he needs his five a day
I think I'll lecture him right away.

When a soldier came into A & E, it was plain to see
[Though he couldn't]
That there was a protrusion sticking out
Affecting half his vision.
For us to pull it out, and save any fuss from
Lawyers 'R Us
They said: Sign on the dotted line to give us your
permission.
Up to that time, things were looking up, it was going fine
But then he took his long last breath, still muttering,
I won't look up next time and where's the dotted line?

A kingly man came to the surgery, removing his crown
discretely
Enquiring about ye DNA, he'd heard about it yesterday,
We had to tell him straightaway,
He need not fret, it hasn't been discovered yet.
Then the Doc said: Is there anything wrong?
Yes, all my relations look the same.
It makes it hard to know their name
We've been marrying first cousins, one another.

I think I'm my uncle or my own half-brother
Doc said: The answer's plain to see
Marry into another dynasty.

This man came into the surgery
He'd been in the orchard hoping to see
A big crunchy apple hanging from the tree.
He saw a biggy, that was russet red
And before he could avoid it, it dropped on his head.
He now has a headache, and one that shouldn't be
Considering he knew its Terminal Velocity.
He started to go cuckoo, then, jumping round the path.
He would have shouted Eureka, if he'd been in the bath.
He started saying silly things, never heard before,
Like, the apple was attracted to the core.
He said: There is this force, a pully-down thing, that you
can't see.
I'm not sure what to call it yet.
In the future he'll probably call it:
That Pully-Down Thing You Can't See, I bet.

In strode this man called Stan
He was Ye Olde Chronicle newspaper man
He'd been wandering round from Med to Cape
He was on a kind of caper, finding a Doc for his paper
As he came in, he said to me: You're Livingstone, I
presume
I said: Oh, no. I only work with the buffoon.
I've told him we can't go on like this

Me in the surgery, him in the wilderness
With his combination of religion and medicine
I'm losing patience. I'm losing patients.

This man hobbled in one day, I guessed he suffered from
piles
But no, it was his feet, he'd been walking for miles and
miles
Now he was a saintly chap from Hibernia, who reckoned he
had an abdominal hernia
You see some old sage had given him a vellum saying:
Truss in the faith if you want to go to heaven.
It was a calligraphic typo. I said: It's not truss it's trust
Now go on your way and preach if you must.

There was a lady in the surgery today,
Who pioneered the use of the first x-ray
She spent considerable energy- alleviating others' misery
Now here's a horrible twist of fate,
One she did not anticipate.
The harm she was doing to herself.
The Doc asked what an x-ray was
She said she would tell him, she would confide
It was a picture of our bones inside.
Now the Doc was nasty without excuse
He said in wartime it might be some use
But in peacetime it will be a fad
It can't be good, it made you bad.

Now in those days, though this sounds insane,
Men thought women had an inferior brain.

The last lot of notes are about a smart Doc.
Now there was a drug that Docs held dear
Not quite a wonder drug but very near
Given to treat a myriad of things
And proving a success in many a sphere
This Doc read reports of babies, born with some
deformity
Instead of seeing, say, one a year; he had seen three
And so he checked with others, looking for a common link
 He found it wasn't parents with genetics on the blink.
He said to other doctors, it's during the nine months I
think
He studied those three mothers in his care
And found out that all three, had taken the same drug
during their pregnancy.
He wrote to the company and to the authorities too.
The company, a powerful one, said: We'll do a review.
Eventually, what the doc said, was found to be true.
By using his gumption he had made the right assumption.
It's a shame more kids were born -
Right up to the time the drug was withdrawn.
I hope the drug companies have now got it:
Always put safety before profit

Melon Man

We were driving in the outback in the Northern
Territory
We drove for miles and miles and miles and miles
Another car, we didn't see.
I saw in the distance what looked like a van
And when we got closer, it was *The Melon Man*
That's what was scrawled on the side of a stall.
Apart from his stall there was nothing there at all.
I said: How is business? He said: I can't complain.
Though I guessed it would be a long time
Before anyone stopped there again.
So we stayed and bought melons and other fruit as well
We made ourselves a picnic of things he had to sell
The Melon Man talked about everything; including this
and that
He said he loved to see people stopping for a chat.
It took another two hours before we left; for sure,
We'd been caught in a trap.
The melons were just a lure.

Mornington's a Happy Place

Mornington's a happy place: so pretty.
Mornington's a happy place: so peaceful.

   The people speak kindly and ask
how you are.
The shops in the main street are sassy
and classy
As you walk down the town to the sea.
If you stop at the top by a shop
It's sunny and peaceful: the walk to the
sea.

Mornington's so happy, so peaceful, so
pretty.

   There's a park by the sea that beckons
and calls
A quiet resting place behind hedges
and walls
But beware. Don't go there. It will lead
to despair
A monument teases and calls you to look.
Ignore it. Go back while you can.
There are names carved in marble
in memoriam

But not from war glory
A different story:
Fifteen young sportsmen all drown,
Coming home from a game.
The grief meant the town would not
be the same.
Mornington's happy if you stop by the
shops.
If you don't read the story, it's all
hunky-dory
But once you've been there, you can't
help but share,
The despair of the parents and friends.
Though the years have gone by,
there are still those that cry
And remember the night of their sorrow.
And they know in their hearts at the end
of the day
That it won't be forgotten tomorrow.

Mornington seems such a happy place.

Love is . . . Everywhere

How many people can you love at once?

Can you love a genius and a dunce?

Why isn't love divided into type?

Is it just a matter of degrees or hype?

Is all love really love or just a tease?

Why can't we name varieties? [like cheese]

[Cheddar love, I thought, would be the family sort]

Maybe we could label love with colours, too

Just liking someone, might be pale blue

Red might be the colour known for lust

Green would be for those we love and trust.

Alas, we have no labels sad to say

So, how do we spot the love that is around

Where love is often hidden, not easily found?

Notice as you wander round today –

Little acts of kindness give it away.

MR POTHOLE

I have a friend I see every day
He's always there for me, not far away
When I see him, I say: Haven't you grown.
Or - Aren't you glad you're not living alone?
And every time I go round that way
He gets bigger and bigger every day.
Then a big rough man begins to shout
I'll fill you in if you don't watch out.
He can't complain. He reached his depth [or peak]
They filled him in. He'll be back next week.

OLD ROBBIE BLARE

Old Robbie Blare was scrupulously fair
With the kiddies gathered round his comfy leather chair
When eating his big blocks of milk chocolate.
He pulled a block from his drawer every day about four
And with a penknife embroidered with pearls
Would scrape up the chocolate in curls.
You could bet a pound or penny that he wouldn't drop any
As the choccy disappeared down his throat.
The kiddies watched on 'til the choccy was gone
And his message, always to explain:
If you give one more than t'other, it might cause some bother.
So with nowt, they're all getting the same.

Robbie Blare

Mrs Prigg and Miss Jolly

It was a regular Saturday for Mrs Prigg and Miss Jolly

They arrived at the Mutual to dish out the Lolly

We were at the Mutual to get money to shop

We thought we'd start early and shop 'til we drop

But there was a queue at the Smartsavers Mutual

Just after nine?

That was really unusual.

To go in, there were two doors, inner and outer

It was a toss up to say, which was stronger or stouter

Miss Jolly was despatched to open the doors

The inner half-opened but would open no more

Mrs Prigg, the manageress, pushed Miss Jolly aside

Saying:

'There's a button between doors, haven't you tried?'

As she squeezed through the gap with elegance and poise

The inner door slammed shut with a squealy type noise

The crowd that had gathered gave a great shout –

Mrs P was in there and couldn't get out.

Miss Jolly to be helpful held up a note, explaining the dilemma

And here's what she wrote:

The doors being electronic and for sure on the blink

If you look you can see they are well out of sync,

But I think I can open both doors just a bit

Thinnest go first, we'll see if you make it.

Then a plump lady, Lily, pushed her way through

'I'm not waiting all day, after you, in the queue'.

Now Mrs Prigg and Lily were both between doors

Pushing and shoving to tremendous applause

Then a little white poodle, who didn't give a jot,

Went up to the doors and wee'd on the lot

After some fizzing and sparking the doors opened wide

With people cheering and rushing inside.

Then Miss Jolly said smugly and with some wit:

'We got the doors open. I knew wee could do it!'

Names

When Roxanne married Mr Stones, she didn't realise
it would cause so many groans.

When Teresa married Mr Green, it began to jar
when people said: I know they are.

J.R.Brown is less self-conscious at registration than
Alan Pratt and Richard Colin Bumstead.

Anne Hathaway wanted a child called Toby.
William wasn't sure of the name or not.

It's your first day in the Languages department
today

Let's get some hoary chestnuts out of the way.

My father didn't suffer from excessive wind, it's
said.

At teatime, Caesar preferred to have sandwich
spread.

If you want to keep up to date,
My French mother's sister uses a ballpoint of late.

Near Miss

- ❖ The penalty and goalpost ping
- ❖ The thrown-back engagement ring
- ❖ The change of mind before the loan
- ❖ The landing just before the drone
- ❖ The flesh wound from the gun attack
- ❖ The bomb gone off before arriving late

WE MORTALS JUST DON'T KNOW OUR FATE

Storm

There's a storm on the way
It's been threatening all day
The storm's getting closer
With crowds speeding home
Driving down highways
Riding down byways
Running down pathways
To sanctuary home.

There's No Place Like Home

INCREDULOUS

Mary's Aunt Alice had sadly passed away
And Mary asked if I'd escort her to the funeral
on that day. We have waited after time: said the
Reverend Edward Emery to those gathered in the chapel
at the cemetery.
The whole of the congregation only numbered four
Mary, myself and Alice's neighbours from next door.
The cemetery was so large it had bus routes running
through. Reverend Edward said: As we seem to be so few
We'll wait awhile, someone may be on the bus at two.
The vicar gave a brief insight into the life that she had
led, and when he spoke about family, he looked at us
instead. He said: Alice had two children.
I was wondering where they could be when the vicar
held up a letter. Now we were going to see:
"Wayne and Sharon wish they could be here with us
To see their Mother interred
But the All Family Lifetime Trip to Vegas Prize
couldn't be deferred."
I thought this was incredulous and I wanted to let them
know – they only had one Mother, someone should
tell them so.
Mary said: You would like to punish them,
No need
They won't forget.
When they come back and think about it,
They'll have a Lifetime Prize of Regret.

First Kiss

The first kiss was soft and quick.
Had I overdone it?
She seemed quite surprised
They said in the book:
You can tell in their eyes
The only thing I noticed, she'd got a stye
I shouldn't have stared,
I made her cry
In desperation, I said:
See you tomorrow
Her face lit up, she forgot her sorrow
And on the second night, I said:
See you tomorrow
A few months went by; she still wasn't sure,
She'd been dumped by lads a few times before.
Then I said:
Do you remember our first kiss?
I never thought it would end like this.
At this she was in tears, looking sad and forlorn.
I said: Oh, I remember our first kiss
I'll remember it forever
I can remember my heart went ping.
The very next morning I bought you this ring.
You can wear it now and forever.

Nicknames

Nicknames can be so much fun
But that doesn't apply to everyone
Some children get upset when labelled with an
epithet.
It is a bit like teasing too
To call someone Thicky or Stinky Poo.
Ask them what name we should call:
That's if they want a nickname at all.

If Only

If only I knew then,
what I know now.
When I thought I knew,
but I didn't know how
I wouldn't have done the things I did
We'd have got on fine
But I didn't know how
Wish I didn't know now
What I didn't know then
We could have started all over again.

My Kids:
four dumplings in a stew

Red Arrows: smoky red, white and blue

Living wage: depends where you live

Inflationary roads: potholes grow quicker than wages

Oral French: careless talk costs grades

Frightfully rich: handbag allowance greater than
average annual wage

Social Service Cuts: social services need social
services

Crime Stats Graph:
x = police cuts, y = stabbings

Nice Story: puppy with winning lottery ticket tucked
in collar rescues kitten from house before gas main
explodes

Thought I'd do one with just one rhyme,
I don't like it
I'll do more next time.

No Mudguards

There was a packer in the bicycle factory
Who thought it was satisfactory
To forget to put mudguards in the boxes.
When he realised, he didn't say.
The batch went away next day.
Then he said he was the one and he told what he had done.
They said: Don't worry, son, they've accepted every one.
The makers must have thought: here's a cost cutting plan.
We'll take away all mudguards if we can.
The packer, expecting the sack,
Found he was getting a pat on the back.
The manufacturers had found, there were dim people around
Who didn't find a wet backside a nuisance in the rain
When they're going for a ride.
They must be thinking:
There's always some daft nut
Let's see, how many other corners we can cut?
If they thought it would work and could get away with it
And if it was possible, they'd make the chain from spit
Now I wouldn't be surprised if we see the day
When they try to take the saddle away
But even a fool would say: A wet and bruised bum?
No way!!!

NOW IS THE TIME

Fat Matt thought it was fun to only eat burgers in a bun
The Doc says: Where's your five-a-day?
Matt said: I don't need them anyway.
He started packing loads of bulk
 People even called him The Incredible Bulk
It took a major medical scare to make him realise and
care.
Now he's on a regime that's mighty tough
But his greens and veggies, he can't get enough
He still has the odd burger, but not all the time
His weight has dropped a little and he's feeling fine.
If you want to change, the time is now, not then
If you don't do it now, we might not see you again.

BE REAL

Those castigating stop and search
Should carry the coffin from the church
It is too late to say we should
Have frisked more people in the neighbourhood.
Shouting about rights and discrimination
Doesn't match the consternation
Of that family standing around
As they lower the coffin into the ground.

Obituary

A nose, a twitching whisker, then a glance
A flashing reconnoitre of the path
Scuttling, rustling, slinking across the lawn
They play among the daisies at the dawn.
Sharp noses, tails of trailing silvery light
Peeping and squeaking, running in the grass
Now all the family's playing ratty games
Busy searching round for frugal crumbs
When darts of light dance through the leaves
and foraging is fun
Oh how life smiles on each and every one
Then bait and traps and every poison known.
And now they're gone
I had half wished that they could stay,
Although I did not really like them anyway.

Obsolete

There is a knacker's yard for words
Thither they go and rest therewith.
They hang sometime upon the skirt
And having chanced a final flirt
They've served their time so gently fade away
Like threepennybit and floppy disk and nay.
It is a right and proper flow
As some words stay and others go.

But some words suffer from a crime
Of dumping them before their time.
Some pedant, scapegrace, what you will
Picks on a word that's not extinct
And drives it to the very brink
By saying 'Do not use this word':
A situation most absurd.

There is a fashion on the go
Suggesting that we do not know
All thespians were called actors, in the past.
Then helpful differentiation came
Lady actors had a name: Actress;
the word so loved and true
But someone said: This just won't do
We ought to make this word taboo
This is a word we will not keep
And others followed on like sheep.

Now when actor Chris lists for audition
They just don't know – it's supposition,
They can't tell if it's a woman or a man.
If Chris puts 'actress' by her name
It surely would be pikestaff plain
That here's a lady for the part, of Tarzan or of
Bonaparte?

Now, what has happened to the oblong word?
The oblong word we recognised
Has suddenly been exorcised.
We looked and named one without second
thought
Four right angles, four sides, two long, two
short
Some modern Maths books now in school
Think that the oblong word's not cool
And call two shapes, just rectangle instead.
Says pavior Fred: Pass a rectangle, Ted.
And Ted passes him a square.
Fred says: You're wrong, I want an oblong.
Now there's a snag that's plain to tell
A square's a rectangle as well.
Ted says: Why didn't you say, it seems we're
wasting half the day?
Why don't you call a spade a spade and then we
will not be delayed?
Ok, said Fred, Now pass the spade.

No, no I meant the shovel.

Now comic words that kids adore
Are demoted to the backroom store
Like zeds, argh, whizz, and arf and blam
While all the kids think they're a laff
The lexicographer thinks they're naff
They are all words that we should see
In any modern dictionary

So if you want words for an early exit
Pick from google, Facebook, Brexit
But better still: those of no use
Those spiteful words: with hate, abuse.

PLASTICS

PLASTIC Plastics

OLWEN GLENDOWER

There was a Welshman called Olwen Glendower
Born a few miles from Swansea, near the Gower
His mother had been hoping for a girl
If she'd had twins
she'd have called one of them, Pearl.
Now Wales is called the Land of My Fathers
But Olwen didn't have one and he thought that
was bad
So when he was twenty, decided to look for his
Dad.

His Mam said: He's Welsh, I'm reasonably sure.
He promised he would visit at the time of the
birth.
To marry me was the intention
And no, I can't remember a face, for what it is
worth
My memory's lost its retention.
Oh, now I remember, I worked it all out.
It could be Taffy from Llandaffy.

Olwen arrived in Llandaffy, one weekend in
September
And went to the local club, as an affiliated
member
News got round the club, they pointed and
whispered:
You see that Lad there, isn't it sad,
He's come to Llandaffy to look for his Dad.

Then one by one, during the morning,
men came to his table, saying
My name's not important, just call me Taffy
I heard of your plight, though I can't put it right
Your Mother must be under some financial stress
Just out of interest, what's your name and
address?

Olwen returned with no joy to be had.
He spoke to lots of Taffys without finding his Dad
But then, most days after that, letters arrived
With a Llandaffy postmark and money inside.

Conversation Tips

If you cannot speak German, it is
surprising and
confusing if you ask if they have children
and they answer: Nein.

Likewise, it is confusing in
the takeaway to ask a
German friend as they are
about to order,
the names that they
have chosen for the twins:
Fritz and Chips.

One O'clock Gun

A Scottish friend said: Have you been
To see a famous Scottish scene?
I think you'll find it rather fun
At Edinburgh Castle you will find –
Sundays excepted –
A ritual you'd have least expected:
The firing of a gun at one.

I was intrigued and so I went to Edinburgh
With intent, to see this world-famous event.
It seems since 1861 a special gun was fired at one.
It may be cynical but fair, to say it lures the
tourists there.
And though it is a strange event, there seems to be
a precedent: a former gun Mons Meg by name
Had in the past, made quite a claim
By blasting gunstone projectiles
a distance of about two miles.
However, those guns were acquiring,
The habit of killing those that were firing,
An historical fact that should not prey
On the minds of the people assembled this day.

We stood expectant on the castle mound
Were warned to stand by for a massive sound.

As tension rose with ten to go;

All eyes were focused on the show

Then, with five minutes left until the fun

A situation, that had not been planned

A man with cleaning rag in hand emerged from
underneath the gun.

While being there, he'd cleaned a label and read a
tag as he was able

Then mumbled to those in command.

The officer heard what had been read

Then stood with utmost calm and said:

Though guns are checked most regularly to spot
defects that there might be

You see this man with rag in hand,

Whilst cleaning, which had not been planned

Has only gone and seen displayed the very year this
gun was made.

This gun will not be fired today,

A new gun we'll facilitate

Until tomorrow you must wait:

This gun is past its shell-by date.

OPS IN A DAY

You know it's time for reckoning, when Auditors
appear in Spring
The last time that the auditors nosed
The staff were cut, some wards were closed.
The money saved would go towards, St Edwards
That edifice of some renown, arising on the edge of
town
For services they'll have to wait.
Completion date is 5 years late

The auditors were experienced and give them their
due
Not only financially but medically too
They saw the new trends as they came into play
And what they liked best, was the ops in a day
That means the patient is not there for a stay; but
all of the action be done in one day.
So they'll tour all the wards, make a hospital scan :
To see which specialisms fit into their plan.

Now 13 wards they had so far seen;
Seeing scope to further their wonderful scheme.
Ward 14 was Swallow ward, with no specialty.
So Swallow ward with irony was put down as not
E.N.T

Now a pattern emerged there throughout the day,
Why ladies were there and why they would stay.
The common story that was told, of shopping,
being in a store,
The next thing, falling to the floor and blacking out
Not knowing that they had been
Transferred by ambulance from the scene
And waking up in ward 14.
Some did have trauma in a way
that could be dealt with in a day
But medical stipulation said: That for a few days
they'd be in bed
Needing care,
not all alone, the very minute they got home.
A person, who would be on hand: a relative or friend.
It is a sad truth that today, in many parts of the UK
Live, lonely old ladies, all alone
Talking only on the telephone.
So if there is no-one there, to comfort and to offer
care,
No matter how quick the op has been, they are going
to stay in ward 14.
Two years later they were dismayed to see
what progress had been made.
The flow, that they had so desired,

was partly there, it had transpired.
But now to make it more perverse, the situation's
even worse
It's just as bad as it had been with overflow from
Ward 14.
They've closed, for ops, wards 1,2,3, and called them
14 a,b,c.
So two years later, it's much the same, the hospital
is full again
With ambulances speeding in each day
With little old ladies, who'll be there to stay.

OUR YVONNE-YVETTE

They are looking for extras at the
House of Horror Films
One of the stipulations in the adverts you'll see:
This is for ordinary people, as ordinary as can be
Mum said: You should try, try, try for that,
our Yvonne
If you don't try, try now, you will never get on.
Long ago, mummy had two auditions; one,
a part in *Moby Dick*
But the thought of the rough seas, made her pukey
and sick.

But she did get a part in *Aladdin and his Lamp*,
She ended up playing the wick.
Then Dad said: What a carry on.
At least it will get you out of the house and into the
House, Yvonne.
And just to boost her confidence Dad said: Don't
worry, Pet,
You're just about as ordinary as anyone can get.
Now Yvonne was no drama queen,
She suffered from low self-esteem .
To make conversation or
talk about the weather
She found it hard
to put two sentences together
Though she could use big words like chastity and
precocious
Her single words and phrases were often quite
atrocious
She was the champion for mixing up a word
Like mupersarket par cark.
She sounded quite absurd.
They arrived at the studios without any hassle
Half the building a palace, the other half a castle.
The scene Yvonne was in, really was the most
dramatic

This had to be the best scene, the director was
emphatic
The last bit when the Zombie arrives,
the climax of the play
The handsome hero is rescuing them:
Will they get away?
The Director then calls Yvonne, Yvette - in fact he
calls her 'Yvette my pet',
The Director says:
It's your turn Yvette, my dear,
It's only three words, now make them crystal clear.
The hero will ask, where will you meet
In the car park or on the street?
Now Yvette, your chance to make your mark
You don't need a script to say:
In the car park.
So the handsome hero shouted,
crystal clear:
Where shall I meet you, then, my dear?
Yvonne then answered, in a tremulous voice:
In the par cark.
The assistant said:
It's wrong. It can go in the bin
The director said:
No, no, we must keep it in.

It was fantastic, the way she looked,
And the way she sounded scared.
For acting of this quality, I hadn't been prepared.
From that day on she built a career and the acting improved her diction.
Now she can talk to anyone with confidence and conviction
Mum and Dad find it hard to call her by her stage name yet
But half-way there; they call her,
Our Yvonne-Yvette.

PAULINE

Pauline Nangle, who liked to be at the centre of things
Decided to call herself Alice Springs.
The reason being, Sydney, her distant relation
Had ended up there after transportation.
Back in England it was a pleasant day in May.
Father and son, Gable and Able Clarke
Took out the old Rover car, to drive round their park.
Into a field they would scamper, with their picnic hamper and chase away their Blues with a dose of countryside views.

Everything was going spiffingly, until, unwittingly,
they saw

A man about to strangle the aforementioned Alice
Springs Nangle.

They recognised the man as Bandy Dilly. You see,

Bandy Dilly

his legs were bowed – that's why they
called him Bandy Dilly.
If he'd been knock-kneed, they would have
called him Knock-kneed Dilly.

Though, personally, I wouldn't have called him that.
I think it sounds rather silly.

They stopped the car and shouted: Stop it,
Unstrangle Miss Nangle.

Bandy replied; I shan't.

Until he noticed the starting handle.

Then he ran into the woods
but no-one gave chase,

Clarke was too old and Able wasn't able.

Don't quote this malicious chat, but I'd say he was
a spoiled brat.

Now after a near strangulation, the pair thought
it their obligation

To take the story for investigation and

Miss Nangle for protection and observation,
to the nearest Police Station.

Then, in the afternoon, picnic over,
they climbed into the Rover and
on the way home, called in to the Police Station
for the latest information.
It appears a likeable fellow, Bandy,
who was passing, which was handy,
would escort the young lady safely back to her home.
He'd said that the first altercation was merely a
demonstration of
how to hold a weasel, not a stoat.
That's why he held Miss Nangle by the throat.
He said he knew, a man of the Sergeant's intellect
Would easily detect
a weasily hold, knowing a stoat hold
was stoatally different.
The Serg was flattered, bamboozled,
taken in, you see;
So he decided he should set the love birds free.
To make it more insane,
as they drove back through the park again,
Alice and Bandy were kissing
beneath a tree.

Able and Clarke were the Author and his Dad

Playing God

Oh, the vet is very helpful and he gives you all the gen
It's the arteries, the liver, the lungs and it's the glands;
you think he'll be decisive but he puts it in your hands
Would you want to be responsible for her misery
and pain?
You want to be decisive but she looks at you again.
That seems to tip the balance you will do what you think's
best:
A life of pain's no option, when you can give her
peace and rest.
Now the vet says, if you want, you can give the fatal dose,
but you want to head back home now;
you are feeling quite morose.
You are driving without feelings and, finally back home:
with sudden consternation you are heading
for the phone.
The phone rings before you get there: when you answer,
it's the vet.
He tells you that the deed is done and it's all for the best:
you've made the right decision and your pet is now at rest.
Then many decades later, as if you would forget,
The password on your laptop brings back memories of your
pet.

Redemption Day

I am proposing, right away, we instigate
Redemption Day
When everyone would wear a suit and written on
the suit would be
A resumé of their life history.
And it would be indicative
Of who you are and how you live
With sections there to indicate
What you love and things you hate
An honest CV of our past
Not for self-aggrandisement with wealth and class
called into play
But with an honest note to call:
to show our true self warts an' all
We'll say bad things are in the past
To get *Redemption Day* at last
We'll look at others with real insight and see them
in a different light.
If only we could have the grace –
The world would be a better place.

THREE DAISIES

How to tell if it's Spring:
It's old country folklore,
To tell if you are not sure
When's the beginning of Spring?
Just go to your lawn, just after dawn
Then wander around and put a foot down
And see how many daisies you cover.
Not two, that won't do, and four is much more,
It's three that marks the beginning.
If still you're not sure, turn on Radio Four
And wait for the news he's announcin'
He'll say: "By the way, Spring starts today."
That saves gettin' outta bed, dunnit.

I AM A FLOWER

I am a flower.
A yellow one.
I gleam and glitter in the sun.
I wake up in the spring.
I am a flower to remind you of
David.
I hear the birds sing.
Do you know who I am?
Pop! I wake from my sleep.
I wear a gleaming, shining dress.
Out of the dark I peep.
I am a daffodil.
Did you guess?

Louise Dowell 1981

THE SCENE OF THE CRIME

The scene of the crime was a Cabinet room.
No poor or homeless were helped at the time.
That was the scene and that was the crime.

The scene of the crime was an outback home.
Natives were cleared from their land at the time.
That was the scene and that was the crime.

The scene of the crime was a drug-filled house.
Young children lived in the house at the time.
That was the scene and that was the crime.

The scene of the crime was a surgical site.
Dogma caused children abuse at the time.
That was the scene and that was the crime.

The scene of the crime was a Syrian town.
Families were bombed in the town at the time.
That was the scene and that was the crime.

The scene of the crime was a workplace of fear.
Bullies controlled the place at the time.
That was the scene and that was the crime.

The scene of the crime was a wire cage.
Pets were kept in the cage at the time.
That was the scene and that was the crime.

The scene of the crime was a hospital corridor.
Patients were waiting for hours at the time.
That was the scene and that was the crime.

The scene of the crime was a widow's house.
Neighbours had left her to die at the time.
That was the scene and that was the crime.

The scene of the crime was a war-time camp.
Arbeit Macht Frei was the lie at the time.
That was the scene: the heinous crime.

The scene of the crime was an Anglian field.
Modern day slaves worked there at the time.
That was the scene and that was the crime.

The scene of the crime was a refugee boat.
Greed would capsize the boat anytime.
That was the scene and that was the crime.

The scene of the crime was a National race.
Horses would die in the race at the time.
That was the scene and that was the crime.

The scene of the crime was a hunting field.
Animals were slaughtered for fun at the time.
That was the scene and that was the crime.

The scene of the crime was a pauper's home.
No hope aspired from the house at the time.
That was the scene and that was the crime.

The scene of the crime was a third world home.
No food at all was there at the time.
That was the scene and that was the crime.

The scene of the crime was a pool of sharks.
Crippling loans were fixed at the time.
That was the scene and that was the crime.

The scene of the crime was an editor's room.
Half-truths and part-news were schemed at the time.
That was the scene and that was the crime.

The scene of the crime was an English town.
Gangs of abusers lurked there at the time.
That was the scene and that was the crime.

The scene of the crime was Speaker's Corner.
People went there to listen and learn.
"You know the trouble with the world today is ignorance
and a lack of compassion. What do you think, sir? "
"I don't know and I don't care."

The scene of the crime was an ordinary house.
One sibling was favoured and given more time.
That was the scene and that was the crime.

The scene of the crime was a hospital ward.
Old folks were stuck in the ward at the time.
That was the scene and that was the crime.

The scene of the crime was a tethered horse.
Meadows were near the horse at the time.
That was the scene and that was the crime.

The scene of the crime was a watering place.
Diseased and rank was the well at the time.
That was the scene and that was the crime.

The scene of the crime was a Passchendaele field.
Young men were wasted, no reason or rhyme.
That was the scene and that was the crime.

The scene of the crime was a sadists' ring.
Tormented animals were there at the time.
That was the scene and that was the crime.

The scene of the crime was an offshore haven.
Taxes avoided there at the time.
That was the scene and that was the crime.

The scene of the crime was a post-war lab.
Ex-Nazi scientists worked there at the time.
That was the scene and that was the crime.

The scene of the crime was a voting booth.
Brexit lies were told at the time.
That was the scene and that was the crime.

The scene of the crime was a restaurant for fads.
Tiny portions were served at the time.
That was the scene and that was the crime.

The scene of the crime was a rendition room.
Victims were tortured there at the time.
That was the scene and that was the crime.

The scene of the crime was a gangland patch.
Members were shot and stabbed at the time.
That was the scene and that was the crime.

The scene of the crime was an old mine field.
Mines were randomly laid at the time
That was the scene and that was the crime.

The scene of the crime was a modern food bank.
The poor were needing food at the time.
That was the scene and that was the crime.

The scene of the crime was a landed estate.
Subsidies added to wealth at the time.
That was the scene and that was the crime.

The scene of the crime was a costly space probe.
Diseases were waiting for cures at the time.
That was the scene and that was the crime.

The scene of the crime was a special chair.
Granny was left in the chair all the time.
That was the scene and that was the crime.

The scene of the crime was a third-world sweatshop.
Children were worked in the place at the time
That was the scene and that was the crime.

The scene of the crime was a factory sweatshop.
Sixteen-hour shifts were worked at the time.
That was the scene and that was the crime.

The scene of the crime was a murderous country.
Guns were available all of the time.
That was the scene and that was the crime.

The scene of the crime was a snobbish club.
Races or genders were banned at the time.
That was the scene and that was the crime.

The scene of the crime had children on shoulders.
Some fell down and were killed at the time.
That was the scene and that was the crime.

"Would you mind helping me? Can you carry this TV on
your shoulder for me? My car is over there."
"Oh no. I might drop it."

The scene of the crime was a new smart motorway.
Families were killed with no safe lane.
That was the scene and that was the shame.

THE SCENE OF THE CRIME WAS A WICKED MIND.
EVIL WAS PLANNED IN THE MIND AT THE TIME.
THAT WAS THE SCENE AND THAT WAS THE CRIME.

Arbeit Macht Frei
'Work sets you free'

The Exceptional Mrs Calfree

When Einstein thought of warped space and time
He must have had Mrs Calfree in mind.
Time as we know it, she just didn't find,
You see Mrs C was as relaxed as could be
Nothing seemed to phase her
She was one of the few people I've found
Who ruled the time in her life; not the other way round.
I'll give you an example.
Wherever she went, she would often arrive late
It was usually accepted without any debate
Those who knew her considered it fate
Though often out of interest they might say:
What is the reason you're late today?
"I saw a dress in a sale. That's what caused the delay."
Sometimes she wore socks, one blue, one grey
If friends said: You seem to have odd socks on today.
Mrs C would laugh and seemed not to care,
Joking: At home, I have a similar pair.
A super-confident woman, hid behind a smiling face
Calmness personified; with kindness and grace

It was hard not to treat her with affection
So she was always accepted as the exception .
Her boss accepted her exception as a small price
to pay
Though lateness and self-assertion might annoy in
some way
Her friends all admired how she lived for the day.
Mrs Calfree was so different. People admired her,
I guess;
Seeing fortitude and calmness alleviated their
stress.
[Missing her vocation: mental health 'ads' NHS?]
She had the knack of knowing what was important or
not
Any pomposity or worry would vanish on the spot.
When I told my daughter how Mrs Calfree could be,
She said: When I am feeling stressed, I'll think of
Mrs C.
Everyone who knew her, suffering from stress,
Should remember her example:
Care-free, but not care-less.

SENT TO COVENTRY
(Just call me Edward, Teddy or Ed)

There's a new boy in school called Edward Defector,
He's been to more schools than an Ofsted
Inspector.
When he arrived at St John's, the first thing he
said:
Just call me Edward, Teddy or Ed. I won't be no
trouble.
Mind you, that's what all of them said.
He came from his last school with some reputation
For nicking and fighting without provocation
The caseworker took him to the Head's office at
nine
I'm calling it office, it was more like a shrine
It was full of mementos of a happier time.
The Head, Miss Hedgerow, gave him the usual chat –
This is how we do things; we don't have any of that.
It took her all day before she knew
Her three gold-topped pens were reduced to two.
And so by the end of his first day at school
He had managed to break every school rule
He spent the whole day thieving and nicking,
Even taking things back if they weren't to his
picking.

He had the usual trouble with his classroom teacher
She admonished him so often, she turned into a
preacher
Tuesday to Thursday, it was the same as before
But Friday Assembly became the last straw.
He sat in assembly and found it a bore
So he left his seat and rolled on the floor.
As he rolled past Miss Hedgerow he knew what he
saw
And shouted the colour of the knickers she wore.
{I won't use the same rhyme; I find it a chore]
Now Miss Hedgerow had lost it. It was easy to tell
When she announced to assembly: "That boy's going
to hell".
That episode with Teddy was all she could bear
She needed him transferred to any place, anywhere.
She knew that his transfer would cause a few sparks
But no-one would have him, not even St Mark's.
The authority decided – it wasn't good news,
He'd stay at St John's until they'd studied reviews.
Now Miss Yawn, an idealist, had originally said;
Oh, look at that Teddy. He looks so divine
If only he was in my class, I'm sure he'd be fine.
Miss Yawn went to the Head who by now was all ears
She knew it was Miss Yawn but even she has ideas.
I'm not just an idealist, I have a plan.

We can change that boy, I'm sure that we can.
I know you will find it hard to believe
But Teddy is lacking the attention he needs.
He needs time in neutral that might do the trick
Not jumping from positive to negative too quick.
We'll send him to Coventry just for a week
We'll starve him of the sort of attention he'd seek.
'Sending to Coventry' is rather strange
You don't actually go there, you just don't engage
You don't acknowledge or try to converse
It meant people ignored him, what could be worse.
By now Teddy was desperate for someone to speak.
This non-attention had lasted nearly a week.
Then on Friday morning, going into school
Callum Chumley forgot the rule
And as Teddy came in through the gate,
Callum Chumley said: Alright, mate?
Now Teddy found a good friend and it worked out
well
Miss Hedgerow even said that he wouldn't go to hell
Teddy has turned over a new leaf and buried the
past
He's a fully-fledged member of the school family at
last.

Scarface : Leanne and Leonie

Leanne and Leonie were pretty little
twins
Though everyone in school knew each name
The way their mum dressed them,
both looked the same.
Even staring hard it was difficult to see
Which one was Leanne and which Leonie.
But one observant teacher noticed the
only clue so far
Just above one of Leanne's eyes was a tiny
jagged scar
You had to peer closely
You could not see it from afar.
So whenever they appeared
the outcome was bizarre,
Someone would get up close, to spot the scar.
Why are you looking at me? Leanne would
say, with surprise.
Now, it would be a disgrace to mention a
scarred face;
So they all had an answer, which was not
even lies:
Leanne, you're a girl with beautiful brown
eyes.

Shirley Sayings

Shirley Sayings knows sayings
She uses them by the score
And as she gets older she uses them more and more.

I just can't wait to see your new date,
What's he like? I said to Shirl on Friday.
You mean my Jack? He's sharp as a tack;
He's the bee's knees; he always aims to please;
He's the icing on the cake, for goodness sake.
I've fallen for him, hook, line and sinker
I'm sure he's a philosopher and thinker.
You ain't seen nothing yet, I'm willing to bet
He's worth his weight in gold.
I'm really sold
I'm walking in sunshine to think that he's all mine
We're a winning combination, it calls for a celebration
He's waiting for the dust to settle, still to show his metal.
Don't know if I said, he's the best thing since sliced bread
I know that he's the one, and he's lots and lots of fun
In fact he's more fun than a barrel-load of monkeys.
He's the cat's whiskers.
I could love him until the cows come home
Think of everything that's great, well that's my new date.

Saw Shirl on Sunday, I couldn't wait to ask about her date.
Don't want to harp on, but I'm glad that he's gone
Call him a man, you gotta be jokin'
Like a jockey without a saddle,

I was up the creek without a paddle
Heading up a blind alley, not heading for Happy Valley
I'll tell it to you straight, in you I can confide
I've been taken for a ride but I'll take it in my stride
He dropped me in it. There's a sucker born every minute.
Stark raving mad, nutty as a fruit cake and by heck
I don't think he was playing with a full deck.
The light was on but I don't think anyone was home

I said: He was not too bright for sure, but that's never
bothered you before.
Was it something that you said, like wanting to be wed?
He was not the marrying kind. It was easy to tell
When I mentioned a ring, he was off like a bat out of hell.
So he slipped through your fingers, Not the one you would
choose?
Now, what's that saying – Some you win, some you lose.

I guessed then Shirley was feeling better when she began to
mutter : Always look on the bright side of life; as one door
closes another one opens; it's an ill wind that blows nobody
any good; she who has the last laugh, laughs longest; if you
spit in one hand and wish in the other, which has the most
in it.

I said Shirley: Calm down.
But then she shouted: I was born within the sound of Bow
Bells
Alright darlin', leave it out, you're 'avin' a larf,
you're 'avin' me on.

I said: Shirley, with all those sayings your brain has gone.
I think your brain is going viral
You've gone into a Cockney Spiral.
There was only one remedy so I thought
Use an old saying that I had been taught
I used it then as the last resort: for Shirley it would work.

*Better to remain silent and be thought a fool than speak
and show you are one*

True love

Sitting there before me:
a love, I love so true
With eyes as brown as moleskin
and lips of russet hue
With skin all soft and peachy,
as soft as honeydew
The one I love so dearly:
Sitting there before me
The one I love is you
I could spend a lifetime thinking
lovely things to say
I'll sit in front of this mirror,
until the end of the day.

SUNDAY TEAS

I met a man in Darwin called
Southern Greg, he was relaxing in a garden
with a stubbie beer.
I asked him: Have you always lived around
here?
He explained in childhood he lived on a
station
But water got scarce, not enough for
irrigation.
It was a large family of thirteen, including
Mom and Dad
He said that he was, always, a happy and
contented lad
And added that the weekend was the best
time to be had.
On Saturday, they all bathed and used the
same water
It started off with Dad and Mom, right
through to the youngest daughter.
Then on Sunday morning: how great it
would be, they'd use the bath water to
make pots of tea.
Greg said: With the cakes, I remember the thrill
Two cups of tea and with luck, a re-fill.
Yummy

Teenage Angst: NO WI-FI

I've just switched on, but the picture's gone
All it says is No Wi-Fi.
Oh, I know what to do, if I can't get through:
Just switch off, then on, all my troubles are gone,
But no, it still says No Wi-Fi.
What does it mean? No Wi-Fi, No Wi-Fi.
Oh, no –
No Facebook. No virtual fun.
No blogs, no pods, no silly sods.
My thousand friends. My mutual friends, My friends
of friends,
No chat, No spat, No hate, No trolls,
I'm in despair if I'm not there.
So I shout and I swear and I say it's not fair:
But a miracle happens before me.
The screen flickers with light. It's a message alright.
It says: Please enter your password.
I've had many a go but computer says:
NO, NO Wi-Fi.
Well, last night in the pub they said
Doug you're a mug,
You're using your name as your password,
So I changed straightaway.
Can't remember today.
It's a town in France or Italy –
or was it Australia – or an
Emisphere: One of them countries.
Still No Wi-Fi.

THIS IS THE WORST DAY OF MY LIFE.

THINKING OF YOU

Ricky Shaw; better known to his friends as Rick
Was caretaker of a school: St Benedict
He was locking up the premises late one night
When a noise in the boiler house gave him a fright
It was TibbyTab the school cat, who'd accidently got
locked in
And seaching for a way out, had knocked over a metal tin
So Rick shooed away Tibby-Tab and had a quick look round
The door had closed behind him and the handle, it had
jammed
And when he tried to force it open, it snapped off
in his hand
It was then that he realised, no matter how he tried,
It was impossible to open from inside.
If he was to be locked in all night, the boiler-room would
do
It's where he kept his food and drink, there even was a loo.
Now there were three boilers; they were controlled
concisely
One was on throughout the night, ambient heating nicely
Two came on to boost the heat at 4.45 precisely.
Rick got hotter during the night, few windows could he use
And so, by midnight, had taken off his shirt and shoes
It wasn't long before he got rid of the rest,
His trousers, socks, underpants and vest,
And lay naked on the floor.
Miss Dalrimple, the headmistress, arrived very early at the
school

The police had made a call to say:

There's graffiti on a wall.

The graffiti read: Miss Dalrimple's a really hot chick.

She saw Rick's car there so she looked for him quick

[For adverby types - ly]

She needed it cleaned up, while it was still dark

In half an hour you would see it from the park.

When she burst into the boiler room there was only one thing on her mind

Go and get as much paint remover as it is possible to find

Rick knew there wasn't enough remover to deal with every brick

So he said: With a lot of paint I'll cover over it.

As people came into the school, they admired the new green wall

Only the police, Rick and Sarah D knew what was underneath it all.

When Rick met Miss D at the end of the day,

With a snigger he started to say:

Remember what the wall said, Sarah:

I think it is true.

As I covered the wall this morning I was thinking only of you.

Then Sarah Dalrimple replied with a cheeky aside:

That's nothing new. I spent the whole day thinking of you.

You don't think I missed that boiler-house view?

Which is better?

Which is better?
Looking out and seeing what is and what
might be -
Or looking in and being sure.
Which is better?

We Are All Unique Like Everyone Else

Why did you say it,
You smarty-pants, know-it-all educationalist?
Once I was different.
You could pick me out in a police lineup from a
Thousand paces.
Everyone knew me for who I was.
Then you came along and threw me on the pile
with all the other old clones.
Shame on you.

Old Folk Lore for Gentlemen

Beware a crowing hen

and a whistling woman

The old adage says:
To Thine Own Self Be True

When Jamie Smitty had reports from school
They always said 'he plays the fool
He causes irritation with his acting and impersonation'.
His parents were concerned he wouldn't get
employment
He wouldn't get a job
He'd end up as a slob
He couldn't even be an actor: his memory was a factor.

When he left school, his Mum and Dad
Thinking he was a caring lad, arranged an interview
At the Palace Home of Residential Care
They said: Be there on Monday for an interview
And whatever you do, don't lark about, just be
yourself.
At the interview Matron said: Your school reports are
vile
They say you are the bottom of the pile. But I
think it's only fair that I'm giving you a trial.
Now Matron, she was caught. She said:
You're better than I thought.
Now Jamie is not always serving tea, though he does
occasionally

Now he wanders from block to block, like a shepherd
tending his flock
If there is laughter and some glee, you know who it
will be.
That's what the residents have found, when Jamie's
been around
They are sitting there in tears, saying: I haven't
laughed like that in years.

One day they had a visit from the Minister of Social
Care
And when she was leaving, ironically, didn't take great
care
She walked into Jamie's tea trolley,
She didn't see it there.
Then Jamie reverted to his real self, for a little while,
Turning to the Minister he said, in Bogart style:
Of all the tea trolleys in the UK she had to walk into
mine.
Then, with a twinkle in her eye, came her reply:
I'm leaving you now, Jamie, but remember: we will
always have Palace.
And so his parents and teachers admitted they were
wrong;
When he acted and larked about, he was being himself
all along.

Trainspotting

For boys and girls of a certain age
Trainspotting, then, was all the rage
Sat on the grass: a motley band
With Ian Allan books in hand
In anticipation, rank on rank
Lined all along the railway bank.
The line belonged to L.M.S.
[If you're not sure what that might be,
look it up and you will see].
There was a time, when this branch line
Was busy, busy as could be,
But then they started cutting back, the line became a single
track.
The station there, a grand affair was derelict
They didn't care.
The place was in a terminal state and no-one seemed to
know its fate.
But then, an irony came into play
It was announced: There was to be, a passenger train just
once a day.
Not Puffing Billy but an express,
and when a locomotive came, there was the chance it bore
a name.
And though the train would pass straight through
For trainspotters like us, 'twould do.
Then not too late, I'd daily wait to see that train: the five
past eight.

At quarter of a mile away, out from a bridge
the engine popped
And we could tell near straightaway the
engine that was on that day
A micky was the worst of all,
A nameless train as I recall,
We'd turn as one and curse and blast and
head for home, or school, downcast.
Yet we would be enthused next day,
At eight o'clock we'd make our way
And yes I do remember still,
anticipation and the thrill
of seeing names we'd never seen before.
There were, however, namers there, that brought
frustration and despair,
And regulars that were a bore,
We'd seen them many times before
Leinster and Munster I recall
And two that were the worst of all
The Fusiliers and Regiments, causing most pain
By returning each week, again and again,
And to show how tense Trainspotting
Became, a quiet six-year-old girl,
I won't say her name,
One time shouted out in frustration and tears
Oh, I hate those bloody fusiliers!

The War to End all Wars

Following the adage:
"Fight Fire with Fire",
Means that we have never learned
That in the end we'll both be burned.
The logic usually ends: Why wait?
Why don't we just proliferate?
We'll end up with a megabomb,
That kills their half of the world in one.
When they see our missile on the way
They will reciprocate and say:
We've pressed our button, cutting it fine.
You also die, you rotten swi ----

Façades

Façades are everywhere
A one-night stand
A regency mansion: riddled with rot, peeling
paper
And stucco that's grot
A rouged cheek with layered make-up
A fat man in a corset
A promise to repay
A smiling face
Woes that cease
A brexit deal, a court of appeal, and
A world at peace

WEB OF LOVE

We fly around looking for aught
As this world spins into an endless arc
And, inadvertently, fly into the web of love
Where we will lose our heart.
Should we just give this web the merest touch
There is an instant to escape its clutch.
Though you think you have escaped this thing
In doing so, you lose a wing
But eventually we'll fly into its deadly trap
On purpose or by slight mishap:
There's no escape.
On its threads there is the glue of love,
'Tis there, but it is hard to see.
Though poets and scholars throughout history
Have sought to unravel its alchemy
It still remains a mystery.
This web becomes an all-consuming thing
And even with a broken string, clings on to all it can.
It is a Tour De Force, that has a happy side of
course.
Some struggle with it, 'til their final breath.
It holds us all, through life, to death.

Wilfrid Cried Wolf

Wilf cried wolf about five times a week,
Although he didn't cry, he gave more of a shriek
While performing a ritual that was quite oblique.
Whatever the chosen scenario, the outcome was the
same.
He had this nasty habit of falling to the floor
With a red-painted neck that looked like gore.
Other times, if it suited, he'd pretend to be
electrocuted.
But each time he'd end up lying still,
feigning death.
Though his teacher and friends had seen it all
before
With the terrifying scream, they knew it was
a ruse, but it did not stop them
shaking in their shoes.
You see his modus operandi was never quite the same
He always had alternatives to brighten up the game.
Now, one week, some visitors were coming to the
school
A wonderful chance for Wilf to play the fool.
Mr Putrid his teacher knew it was time to act,
I guess.

He couldn't risk Wilf causing visitors distress
So he called on his friends Bill and Chris to lend a hand
To give him some help with an idea he had planned.
Bill went to the school, in the afternoon, next day
It wasn't very long before Wilf started his display.
Bill said: I'm concerned.
I'll call for an expert right away.
The next thing that happened Wilf was saying:
I'm OK.
When expert Chris arrived, Mr Putrid asked:
What do you suggest?
Chris said after a shock like that he needs a perfect rest
He'll stay in bed the whole weekend.
I think that will be best.
His parents will see it's the only remedy.
Now with an expert on his case, Wilf decided to change face.
"I'll stop playing silly tricks," he said,
"I'll stop pretending to be dead.
If only I can have my weekends free I'll be as good as I can be".
   He never played those silly tricks again.

WOMEN OF THE NORTHERN TERRITORY

I rested in the blazing sun, in the park,
Parched and dusty, a need to unwind.
Then the women came.
The Women of the Northern Territory
The Women of the Northern Territory rallying
The Women of the Northern Territory talking
The Women of the Northern Territory droning
And whining
The drone of mutual back-slapping
Margaret's service to state politics
Val's service to local politics
No effort beyond scrutiny
Leave? Why should I? I was here first
But hark – the interlude
The Didgeridoo player – synthetic not authentic
A white youth, an electric Didg
Too much.
I crawl away, like a wounded animal
To rest in peace.

Nearing Sports Day

There was a kid in our school called

Soapy Hope

He could run like the wind.

The week before Sports day,

he took a tube of Germylean to school

to put on his sore knee

The local chemist witnessed a run,

that emptied his Germylean stock,

He made quite a killing you see.

So when the next week Soapy decided

to put on a plaster

The chemist prayed most fervently:

Don't let Soapy tell the other kids.

A PLASTER WON'T MAKE YOU RUN ANY FASTER.

*

SPELLING

My teacher tells me: my spelling needs improving slightly.

If I spelled prefect, it would be perfect.

Wedding Dreams

Phil and I were teenage friends, friends of the groom
We'd been invited to the wedding one Saturday in June.

Finding the venue, in that Northern town
really was a game: looking out for landmarks
when those terraced streets looked all the same.
But we arrived at the bride's mother's; Maureen
was her name.

She said: Leave it there, if that's your car - the
walk to the church isn't very far.
Now, which one of you is Phillip? You go inside;
the bathroom's upstairs; there's a label on your
bedroom door;
Be back out here in five minutes and not a
minute more.

Now your friend can sleep at Mrs Bradshaw's
place - so come along now, let's show your face.
When we knocked on Mrs Bradshaw's door, a
voice said: Come on in,
So you've come for the wedding,
I'll show you your room.
Enjoy the reception and don't come back too
Soon. Don't worry about not getting in, we don't
lock our doors at all.

There's nowt worth pinching around here and
some folk leave their dog in the hall.

Before we left for the church, Maureen said to me
Be here in the morning for some breakfast and
some tea.
I thought we could meet together and get to
know each family.

The wedding was just like they wanted it to be
The Happy Couple were very, very happy.
I looked at Steve; he looked really pleased
In a year or two, he might be changing a nappy.

At the disco that evening, the two bridesmaids
were there.
We came to the conclusion, they were definitely
fair
We had had a few drinks and we started to
compare - Penny was forthcoming and Elise was a
tease
Both said they had no boyfriend to put us at our
ease
But the way they began to mingle they couldn't
possibly be single and both were nearly eighteen.
Though we knew they were not fair game, we
enjoyed dancing with them just the same.

After midnight, I tip-toed back, all I wanted to
do now was to rest my head.
In the bedroom I pulled off my clothes, and in

the dimness, I slipped into bed.
Now, I'd had a few drinks so I wasn't quite sure,
After a while, I thought I must be dreaming.
Just then I heard a sigh and a warm hand was
touching my thigh.
O what a dream and what a tease; it must be
Elise.
But then, a voice boomed out, I sat up
straightaway and heard a lady say:
You must be with the wedding party.
I think you want Mrs Bradshaw, the lady next
door,
You should be round there at number twenty-
four.
The dream ended. I panicked. I shot out of bed.
Quickly got dressed, said Thank You, then fled.
Next morning at Maureen's the night was a blur
I thought I remembered but couldn't be sure.

Then Ruth, an elderly lady, who had just popped
in, said:
You'll never guess what happened: and started
to grin.
When she told her story it had a familiar ring,
But the others said: Ruth, you must have been
dreaming or the Babycham had kicked in.
Then Elise, who had listened, said: I had the
same dream but the man stayed on and things
started to steam.

On the journey home Phil got inquisitive and
started to shout: You know you're a sly one.
Last night, it was you she was talking about.
It wasn't a dream. Is it true?
I said: Phil, I'll admit it. It was me. That's the
truth.
I thought he was talking about the incident with
Ruth
But he said; You rascal. Did Elise live quite close?
She's a beautiful girl. You must have had a ball
It's a wonder you came back at all.

To this day he believes I had a steamy night with
Elise,
I have been unfurled as a smooth operator; a
man of the world
Phil seeks my advice about affairs of the heart.
Affairs of the heart? I wouldn't know where to
start,
He sees me as some sort of mentor.
Now if he had asked me at the time, I would have
said
He still doesn't know but I won't tell him so - I
have to keep up my street cred.

You're Talking Baloney

If Grandad said: It's getting worse
Get on the blower and ring for a hearse
I don't think there's any more I can give
I think I'm losing the will to live.
I'd say to Gramps:

You're talking Baloney

Before you pegged out you'd be saying 'if only'.
It's your birthday tomorrow, one hundred and
two
Let's think of some things that you could do
Tonight we'll go to the gala bingo
And on the way we'll stop
And spend a hundred quid in the betting shop.
And then there's that ninety-year-old Nancy
The one you said you really fancy.
Take her to the Palais at the end of the alley
Take her to the dance, it might lead to romance
Take her out to dine, with food and wine
Then if you say you're still sad and lonely
I'll repeat what I said:

You're talking Baloney

Printed by: Copytech (UK) Limited trading as
Printondemand-worldwide.com
9 Culley Court, Bakewell Road, Orton Southgate,
Peterborough, PE2 6XD